Antonio Sant'Elia

Antonio Sant'Elia

Antonio Sant'Elia

teNeues

Editor in chief:
Paco Asensio

Archipockets coordination:
Aurora Cuito

Editor and original texts:
Llorenç Bonet

Drawings:
All drawings belong to Museo Civico. Comune di Como.
Musei Civici, Pinacoteca Civica.

English translation:
William Bain

German translation:
Susanne Meraner

French translation:
Agencia Lingo Sense

Italian translation:
Giovanna Carnevali

Graphic design / Layout:
Emma Termes Parera and Soti Mas-Bagà

Published worldwide by teNeues Publishing Group
(except Spain, Portugal and South-America):

teNeues Book Division
Kaistraße 18, 40221 Düsseldorf, Germany
Tel.: 0049-(0)211-994597-0
Fax: 0049-(0)211-994597-40

teNeues Publishing Company
16 West 22nd Street, New York, N.Y., 10010, USA
Tel.: 001-212-627-9090
Fax: 001-212-627-9511

teNeues Publishing UK Ltd.
Aldwych House, 81 Aldwych
London WC2B 4HP, UK
Tel.: 0044-1892-837-171
Fax: 0044-1892-837-272

teNeues France S.A.R.L.
140, rue de la Croix Nivert
75015 Paris, France
Tel.: 0033-1-5576-6205
Fax: 0033-1-5576-6419

www.teneues.com

Editorial project:

© 2003 LOFT Publications
Domènech 7-9, 2o 2ª
08012 Barcelona, Spain
Tel.: 0034 932 183 099
Fax: 0034 932 370 060
e-mail: loft@loftpublications.com
www.loftpublications.com

Printed by:
Gráficas Anman. Sabadell, Spain.

February 2003

Bibliographic information published by Die Deutsche Bibliothek
Die Deutsche Bibliothek lists this publication in the Deutsche Nationalbibliografie;
detailed bibliographic data is available in the Internet at http://dnb.ddb.de.

ISBN: 3-8238-5547-6

12 Under the Sign of Otto Wagner

24 Cassa di Risparmio

30 Monumental Buildings

38 Electric Power Plants

44 Architectural Elements

52 Industrial Buildings

60 Theaters

66 La Città Nuova

74 Metropolitan Churches

78 Chronology

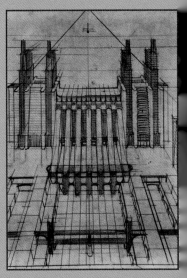

Antonio Sant'Elia was born in the Italian city of Como in 1888 and died, at the age of 26, fighting on the front line in World War I. In spite of hardly ever having worked in his profession, his drawings have, over the course of the twentieth century, captivated different generations of architects. And his 1914 manifesto of Futurist architecture is the first text of the historical avant-garde to set forth a renovation of the architectural culture.

Sant'Elia acquired his technical know-how in the Castellani School of Fine Arts in Como, specializing in civic architecture, hydraulics, and road building. In 1907, he moved to Milan, and there established his first contact with avant-garde movements, specifically with the Futurists, followers of Marinetti. This tendency, which began as a literary movement and swiftly spread to other spheres, was the platform and the cultural backdrop from which Sant'Elia went about creating his proposals. In fact, Futurism was more an intellectual attitude than a concrete artistic program—even though there existed a widely shared idea of modernity, one which tended to exalt the concepts of machine, city, dynamism, and the future, contrasting these to the idea of the past, bourgeois society, the museum, or the library. Futurism will in fact constitute the first avant-garde movement that attempts to define, in all artistic fields, that which fits into its vision of modernity. In 1909, Marinetti will publish the first manifesto—including the famous phrase "a racing car [...] is more beautiful than the Victory of Samothrace"—following it with a second manifesto on painting (1910), then a third, on sculpture (1912). These precedents will then in turn be followed by the appearance of the manifesto on architecture, signed by Sant'Elia and revised by Marinetti in the first edition.

Somewhat after the fashion of Adolf Loos (Ornament and Crime, 1908), the great precursor of rationalism, Sant'Elia affirms that the repertories of the past are incongruent in the context of modern society and that architecture must exploit the new materials—iron and concrete—without recourse to the language of the past. He also defends the need to develop an ephemeral architecture so that each generation can build the city of its needs.

From the manifesto and from his drawings comes Sant'Elia's concern with modernizing the cities on the basis of an idea of the great metropolis based on communications and energy: electric power plants, airports, and railroad stations, wireless communications, factories, and high-rise houses are the subjects of his pictures. And they are framed in an industrial Milan, but one which still is moved basically by animal energy, coal, and gas.

In spite of sharing certain concerns and solutions with the later modern architectural movement, the configurations proposed by Sant'Elia owe no small debt to his own recent past, that is, both to the Viennese Secession of Otto Wagner and his successors as well as to the industrial projects of Tony Garnier, or the vision of the New York of the first decade of the last century. Sant'Elia's drawings will arise as visual approximations more than true architectural projects: rarely do there appear ground plans and elevations, and what predominates is a monumentalism of forms over their practicality, use, or planning in any real given environment. This is largely what distances him from the later rationalist positions.

In spite of this anachronism, the Como architect's proposals are revolutionary and delineate the transition toward a new era. Indeed, the work of Sant'Elia, along with the Fritz Lang film "Metropolis" (1927), comprise a highly potent twentieth-century image of the modern city.

Antonio Sant'Elia wurde 1888 in der italienischen Stadt Como geboren und fiel im Ersten Weltkrieg im Alter von 26 Jahren an der Front. Obwohl er seinen Beruf kaum ausüben konnte, begeisterten seine Skizzen während des 20. Jahrhunderts verschiedene Generationen von Architekten und sein Manifest zur futuristischen Architektur von 1914 stellt den ersten Text der historischen Avantgarde dar, der eine Erneuerung der Kultur der städtischen Institutionen forderte.

Sant'Elia erlangte seine technischen Kenntnisse im Fachgebiet Zivilbauten, Wasserbau und Straßenbau an der Kunsthochschule Castellani in Como. 1907 zog er nach Mailand um, wo er ersten Kontakt mit der Avantgarde, genauer gesagt mit den Futuristen, den Anhängern Marinettis, aufnahm. Diese Strömung, die als literarische Bewegung anfing und sich dann schnell in anderen künstlerischen Bereichen verbreitete, war das Sprungbrett und der kulturelle Hintergrund für die Ausarbeitung der Vorschläge Sant'Elias. Der Futurismus war eigentlich eher eine intellektuelle Haltung als ein konkretes künstlerisches Programm, obwohl eine mehrheitlich einstimmige Vorstellung der Modernität bestand, welche die Begriffe Maschine, Stadt,

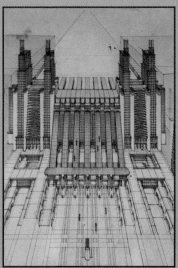

Cemetery (Como, Italy)
Friedhof (Como, Italien)
Cimetière (Como, Italie)
Cimitero (Como, Italia)

Villa Elisi (Como, Italy)
Villa Elisi (Como, Italien)
Villa Elisi (Como, Italie)
Villa Elisi (Como, Italia)

The tomb (Monza, Italy)
Das Grab (Monza, Italien)
La tombe (Monza, Italie)
La tomba (Monza, Italia)

Dynamismus und Zukunft pries und diese der Idee von Vergangenheit, Bourgeoisie, Museum oder Bibliothek entgegenstellte. Als erste avantgardistische Bewegung strebte der Futurismus danach, seine Vorstellung von Modernität in allen Bereichen der Kunst zu verwirklichen. 1909 veröffentlichte Marinetti das erste futuristische Manifest, in dem sein berühmter Satz „ein Rennwagen ist schöner als die Nike von Samothrake" erscheint. Danach folgten das Manifest der Malerei (1910) und das Manifest der Skulptur (1912), die dem Manifest der futuristischen Architektur vorausgingen, welches Sant'Elia unterzeichnete und das Marinetti in der ersten Auflage überarbeitete.

Ebenso wie Adolf Loos (Ornament und Verbrechen, 1908), der große Vorgänger des Rationalismus, behauptete Sant'Elia, dass die Stilelemente der Vergangenheit mit der modernen Gesellschaft unvereinbar sind und dass die Architektur die neuen Baumaterialien Eisen und Beton nutzen solle, ohne auf die Ausdrucksformen der Vergangenheit zurückzugreifen. Er verteidigte auch die Idee der Kurzlebigkeit der Architektur, nach der sich jede Generation ihre eigene Stadt nach ihren Bedürfnissen bauen könne.

Das Manifest und seine Zeichnungen zeigen das Anliegen Sant'Elias, die Städte zu modernisieren, ausgehend von der Vorstellung der großen Weltstadt der Verkehrswege und der Energie: Elektrizitätswerke, Flughäfen und Bahnhöfe, drahtloses Fernmeldewesen, Fabriken und Hochhäuser bilden die Schwerpunkte seiner Zeichnungen, die das industrielle Mailand umgeben, das im Grunde noch immer durch Zugtiere, Kohle und Gas betrieben wurde.

Obwohl er Anliegen und Lösungen mit der nachfolgenden modernen Architekturrichtung teilte, haben die von Sant'Elia vorgeschlagenen Formen viel der jüngsten Vergangenheit zu verdanken, sowohl der Wiener Secession Otto Wagners und seiner Nachfolger als auch den Industrieprojekten Tony Garniers oder der Vision New Yorks Anfang des vorigen Jahrhunderts. Seine Zeichnungen sind eher visuelle Annäherungen als architektonische Projekte: sehr selten enthalten sie Grundrisse und Ansichten, der vorherrschende Monumentalismus der Formen geht über Zweckmäßigkeit, Brauchbarkeit oder Planung der Umgebung hinaus, was ihn sehr von der Haltung der Rationalisten entfernt.

Trotz dieses Anachronismus' sind die Vorschläge des Architekten aus Como revolutionär und prägen den Übergang zu einer neuen Epoche. Tatsächlich bildet das Werk Sant'Elias', gemeinsam mit dem Film „Metropolis" von Fritz Lang (1927), die größte Utopie der modernen Stadt des 20. Jahrhunderts.

Antonio Sant'Elia est né dans la ville italienne de Côme, en 1888, et mourut à 26 ans en combattant au front lors de première guerre mondiale. Bien qu'il ait peu exercé sa profession, ses dessins ont captivé plusieurs générations d'architectes tout au long du XXème siècle. Son manifeste de l'architecture futuriste de 1914 a d'ailleurs constitué le premier texte des avant-gardes historiques, amorçant le débat de la rénovation de la culture architecturale.

Sant'Elia acquiert ses connaissances techniques à l'école des Beaux-Arts Castellani de Côme, dans la spécialité du génie civil, hydraulique et routier. Il déménage pour Milan en 1907, établissant alors ses premiers contacts avec les avant-gardistes et, plus concrètement, avec les futuristes, disciples de Marinetti. Ce courant, apparu tout d'abord sous la forme d'un mouvement littéraire, s'est propagé rapidement aux autres sphères, constituant à la fois la plate-forme et l'arrière plan culturel selon lesquels Sant'Elia élabora ses propositions. De fait, le futurisme fut plutôt une attitude intellectuelle qu'un programme artistique concret. Naissait une idée de modernité largement consensuelle et exaltant les concepts de machine, cité, dynamisme et futur, en contrepoint de notions comme le passé, la société bourgeoise, le musée ou la bibliothèque. Le futurisme constitue le premier mouvement avant-gardiste tentant de définir, dans tous les domaines artistiques, sa vision propre de la modernité. En 1909, Marinetti publie le premier manifeste – où apparaît sa célèbre phrase « une automobile rugissante [...] est plus belle que la Victoire de Samothrace » – qui sera suivi par ceux de la peinture (1910) et de la sculpture (1912) précédant celui de l'architecture, signé par Sant'Elia et révisé par Marinetti lors de sa première édition.

À l'image d'un Adolf Loos (Ornement et crime, 1908), le grand précurseur du rationalisme, Sant'Elia affirme que les références au passé sont une absurdité dans le contexte de la société moderne et que l'architecture doit exploiter les nouveaux matériaux – le fer et le béton – sans recourir à un langage passéiste. Il défend également le développement impératif d'une architecture de l'éphémère afin que chaque génération puisse construire la cité selon ses nécessités.

Du manifeste et de ses dessins émane la préoccupation de Sant'Elia pour la modernisation des villes, fondée sur l'idée de la grande métropole reposant sur la communi-

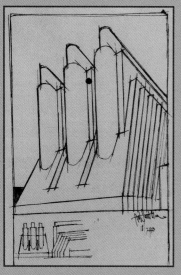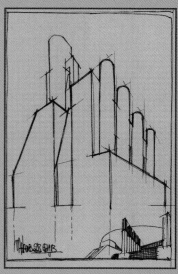

cation et l'énergie : les centrales électriques, les aéroports et les stations de chemin de fer, les communications sans fil, les usines et le logement en hauteur sont les thèmes de ses croquis. Ils peuplent un Milan industriel mais vivant encore essentiellement au rythme de la traction animale, du charbon et du gaz.

Bien qu'il ait partagé les attentes et les solutions du mouvement moderne architectural postérieur, les formes envisagées par Sant'Elia doivent beaucoup à son passé récent, à la Secession viennoise d'Otto Wagner et de ses successeurs mais aussi aux projets industriels de Tony Garnier voire à la vision new-yorkaise de la première décennie du XXème siècle. Ses dessins constituent des approches visuelles plus que de réels projets architecturaux : niveaux et élévations sont peu souvent apparents et le monumentalisme prédomine les formes au-delà de la pratique, de l'usage ou de la planification quant à l'environnement. Il s'écarte ainsi largement des positions rationalistes ultérieures.

En dépit de cet anachronisme, les propositions de l'architecte de Côme sont révolutionnaires et marquent la transition vers une nouvelle ère. De fait, l'œuvre de Sant'Elia, à l'unisson du film de Fritz Lang « Metropolis » (1927), forme l'imaginaire le plus puissant du XXème siècle pour la cité moderne.

Antonio Sant'Elia é nato nel 1888 nella cittadina italiana di Como e morì con appena 26 anni durante la prima Guerra Mondiale combattendo sul fronte. Anche se esercitò pochissimo la sua professione, i suoi disegni hanno affascinato differenti generazioni di architetti lungo tutto il XX° secolo, ed il suo manifesto dell'architettura futurista datato nel 1914 costituì il primo testo delle avanguardie storiche della cultura architettonica.

Sant'Elia acquisisce la propria formazione tecnica presso la Scuola di Belle Arti Castellani di Como, specializzandosi in edilizia, ingegneria idraulica e civile. Nel 1907 si trasferisce a Milano, periodo in cui entra in contatto con le avanguardie, in particolar modo con i futuristi, seguaci di Marinetti. Questa corrente ebbe inizio da un movimento letterario che si diffuse rapidamente in altre sfere; fu la piattaforma e lo sfondo culturale grazie al quale Sant'Elia elaborò le sue proposte. Infatti il Futurismo venne considerato maggiormente come un movimento intellettuale piuttosto che con un programma artistico concreto, anche se esisteva un'idea basata su una modernità consenziente nell'esaltare il concetto della macchina, della città, del dinamismo e del futuro, contrapponendola con l'idea del passato, della società borghese, del museo o della biblioteca. Il Futurismo costituisce il primo movimento di avanguardia che intenta di definire, in tutti i campi delle arti, la sua visione della modernità. Nel 1909 Marinetti pubblica il primo manifesto dove appare la sua famosa frase "un bolide di strada é più affascinante della Vittoria di Samotracia", al quale seguiranno i dipinti (1910) e le sculture (1912), precedenti all'architettura, firmata da Sant'Elia e di cui Marinetti ritoccò nella prima edizione.

Come accadde ad Adolf Loos (Ornamento e delitto, 1908), il grande precursore del razionalismo, Sant'Elia dichiara che i repertori del passato sono un'incongruenza con il contesto della società moderna, e che l'architettura deve sfruttare i nuovi material – il ferro e il cemento – senza dover ricorrere al linguaggio del passato. Difende inoltre la necessità di sviluppare un'architettura effimera affinché ciascuna generazione possa costruire la città secondo le proprie necessità.

Dal manifesto ai suoi disegni si slega la preoccupazione di Sant'Elia di modernizzare le città a partire dall'idea di una grande metropoli basata sula comunicazione e sull'energia: le centrali elettriche, gli aeroporti, le stazioni ferroviarie, le comunicazioni inalambriche, le fabbriche, gli edifici residenziali sviluppati in altezza sono i temi dei suoi disegni che si inquardrano in una Milano industriale che si muove ancora con trazione animale, carbone e gas.

Non ostante condivide le preoccupazioni e le soluzioni con il posteriore movimento architettonico moderno, le forme proposte da Sant'Elia riflettono molto il proprio passato recente, dalla Secessione Viennese di Otto Wagner ai suoi successori così come ai progetti industriali di Tony Garnier o la visione di New York del primo decennio del secolo scorso. I suoi disegni costituiscono approssimazioni visuali piuttosto che progetti architettonici: molto raramente appaiono piante e prospetti, mentre predomina il monumentalismo delle forme sulla praticità, l'uso o la pianificazione dell'intorno, il che lo allontana abbastanza dalle prese di posizioni razionaliste successivamente adottate.

Non ostante l'anacronismo, le proposte dell'architetto di Como sono rivoluzionarie e marcano il passaggio verso una nuova epoca. Di fatto, il lavoro di Sant'Elia, insieme al film "Metropolis" di Fritz Lang (1927), definiscono l'immaginario più potente del XX° secolo della città moderna.

Under the Sign of Otto Wagner

The first works of Sant'Elia are deeply marked by the eclectic style of the beginning of the twentieth century, and influenced in no small measure by the work of Otto Wagner and his successors. Sant'Elia's preference for this architecture characterizes all of his mausoleum pieces, including the cemetery he planned in 1916 for the victims of his military unit, the Arezzo Brigade, where he himself was also buried. Sant'Elia recurs to the patterns of Viennese Art Nouveau because these are more accepted by the public than is the innovative line with which he will experiment in parallel, but also because of a personal preference. Even the project for the Milan railroad station he entered in a 1912 competition (at a time when he had been researching new architectural forms for more than three years) will show an obvious debt to the teachings of Wagner—above all the earliest. The project for Monza cemetery plays with the grandiloquent designs of Art Nouveau and presents many symbols (cypresses, fallen anthropomorphic sculptures, moldings that create powerful chiaroscuros). The human figures that appear in these pictures show the refinement and the delicacy of their conception, rather distanced from the manner in which he would present these figures from 1914.

Die ersten Werke Sant'Elias' waren stark vom eklektischen Stil der Jahrhundertwende geprägt und sehr vom Werk Otto Wagners und dessen Nachfolgern beeinflusst. Seine Vorliebe für diese Architekturform kennzeichnet seine gesamten Grabwerke, eingeschlossen der Friedhof, den er 1916 für die Opfer seiner Militäreinheit – die Brigade Arezzo – plante und wo auch er bestattet wurde. Sant'Elia griff auf die Formen des Wiener Jugendstils zurück, da diese in der Öffentlichkeit mehr Akzeptanz fanden als die erneuernde Linie, die er parallel dazu erprobte, aber auch aus persönlicher Vorliebe. Sogar am Projekt für das Mailänder Bahnhofsgebäude, das er 1912 zur Ausschreibung präsentierte, nachdem er schon über drei Jahre neue architektonische Formen erforschte, erkennt man, dass er vor allem den frühen Lehren Wagners verpflichtet war. Das Projekt für den Friedhof von Monza spielt mit den bombastischen Formen des Art nouveau und weist zahlreiche Symbolismen auf: Zypressen, liegende anthropomorphe Skulpturen, Simse, die starke Helldunkeleffekte erzeugen. Die menschlichen Figuren auf diesen Zeichnungen zeigen das Raffinement und die Feinfühligkeit der Konzeption, weit entfernt von der Art und Weise, wie die Figuren ab 1914 dargestellt werden.

Les premières œuvres de Sant'Elia sont profondément marquées par le style éclectique du début du siècle et sous l'influence des travaux d'Otto Wagner et de ses disciples. Sa préférence pour cette architecture caractérise toute sa production funéraire, y compris le cimetière projeté en 1916 pour les victimes de son unité militaire – la brigade Arezzo – et où il fut lui-même inhumé. Sant'Elia fait appel aux formes de l'Art Nouveau viennois, car mieux acceptées par le public que la ligne novatrice qu'il expérimente en parallèle, mais aussi par goût personnel. Même le projet de la gare ferroviaire de Milan, qu'il présente en 1912, alors qu'il effectuait des recherches depuis plus de trois ans sur de nouvelles formes architecturales, affiche une dette envers les enseignements de Wagner, surtout les plus précoces. Le projet du cimetière de Monza joue avec les formes grandiloquentes de l'Art Nouveau, présentant de nombreux symbolismes – cyprès, sculptures anthropomorphiques, moulures créant de puissants clairs-obscurs. Les représentations humaines apparaissant dans ces dessins font montre du raffinement et de la délicatesse de leur conception, notablement éloignée des formes figuratives existantes en 1914.

I primi lavori di Sant'Elia sono profondamente marcati da uno stile eclettico dell'inizio secolo, e risultano molto influenzati dalle opere di Otto Wagner e dai suoi successori. La sua predilezione per questa architettura caratterizza tutta la produzione funeraria, incluso il cimitero che progettò nel 1916 per le vittime del suo plotone militare, la brigata di Arezzo, dove venne anch'egli interrato. Sant'Elia utilizza forme dell'art nouveau viennese in quanto maggiormente accettate del pubblico, piuttosto che la linea innovatrice che sta sperimentando in parallelo, anche per decisione personale. Per lo stesso motivo anche la stazione ferroviaria di Milano che presentò al concorso del 1912, quando ormai era al terzo anno di sperimentazione di nuove forme architettoniche, dimostra dubbi riguardo gli insegnamenti di Wagner, specialmente i primi. Il progetto per il cimitero di Monza gioca con le forme magniloquenti dell'art nouveau e presenta numerosi simbolismi – cipressi, sculture antromorfiche abbattute, forme che dimostrano la raffinatezza e la delicatezza della sua concezione, abbastanza lontana dalla forma di rappresentare queste figure a partire dal 1914.

PARTICOLARE

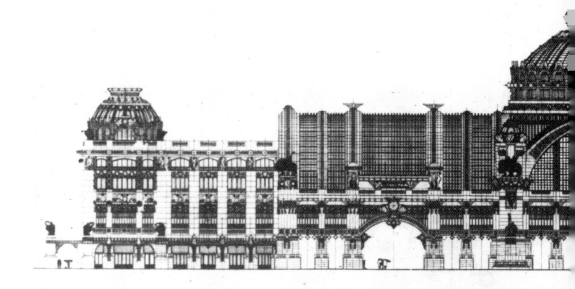

FACCIATA P

On the project for the central railroad station in Milan, an eclectic repertory was used, with the aim of creating a monumental edifice, as these drawings and those on the preceding page show.

So wie es die Bilder dieser und der vorherigen Seite zeigen, benutzte er beim Projekt für den Hauptbahnhof von Mailand ein eklektisches Repertoire, um ein monumentales Gebäude zu errichten.

Pour le projet de la Gare centrale de Milan, il utilise un répertoire éclectique dans l'intention de créer un édifice monumental, comme le montrent ces dessins et ceux de la page précédente.

Nel progetto per la stazione Centrale di Milano utilizza un repertorio eclettico, con l'obiettivo di creare un edificio monumentale, come rappresentano questi disegni e quelli della pagina anteriore.

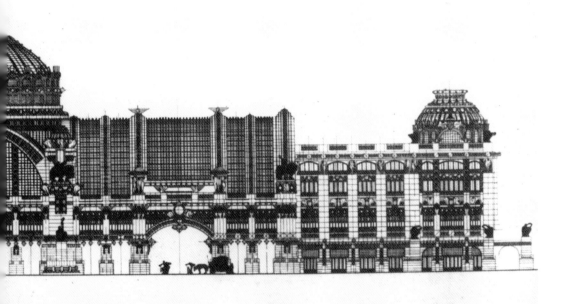

PALE 1:200

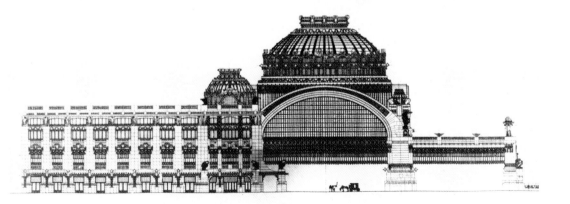

This project for a kiosk with a masculine figure shows the technical mastery and the personality of Sant'Elia's draftsmanship, as in the plan for the Società Comessi (right), or the drawing of a façade at the beginning of this chapter.

Dieses Projekt eines Kiosks mit einer männlichen Figur zeigt das Know-how und die Persönlichkeit der Zeichnung Sant'Elias, genauso wie der Entwurf für die Società Comessi rechts oder die Zeichnung der Fassade, mit welcher das Kapitel eröffnet wird.

Ce projet de kiosque comportant une représentation masculine prouve la maîtrise et le caractère du dessin de Sant'Elia, comme le projet pour la Società Comessi, à droite, ou le croquis de la façade ouvrant ce chapitre.

Questo progetto del chiosco con un'immagine maschile dimostra il predominio e la personalità del disegno di Sant'Elia, così come il progetto per la Società Comessi, a destra, o il disegno di una facciata che apre questo capitolo.

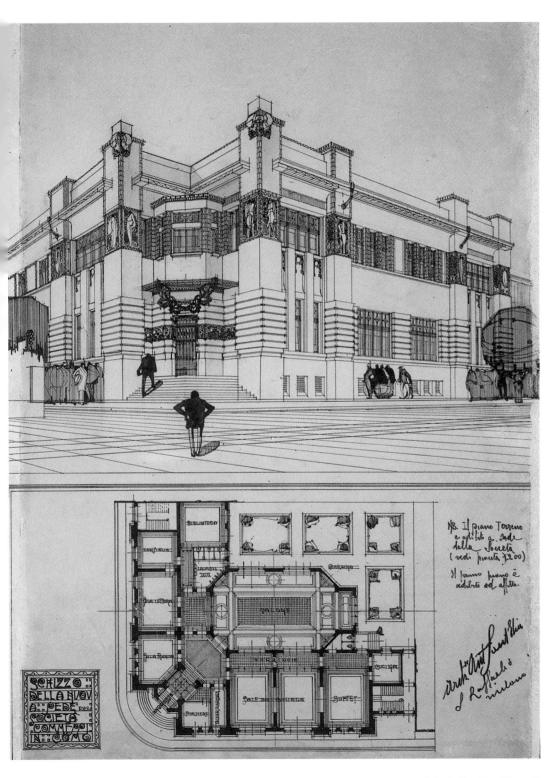

Arch. ANTONIO SA...
· 30-4-1888 · 10-10-1·

22 Under the Sign of Otto Wagner

The project for Monza cemetery surprised the jury, who praised the originality of the drawings in spite of not awarding it an honorable mention. On the preceding page, a sketch for the same dossier is seen with a preparatory drawing for the plaque and small gravestone monument of Gerardo Caprotti (1914), in the same cemetery.

Die Ausfertigung für den Friedhof von Monza überraschte die Jury, die die Originalität hervorhob, obwohl sie ihm keinen Trostpreis anerkannte. Auf der vorherigen Seite sieht man eine Skizze für dasselbe Projekt, gemeinsam mit einer Zeichnung für das Grabmal von Gerardo Caprotti (1914), das sich auf dem gleichen Friedhof befindet.

Le projet pour le cimetière de Monza surprit le jury, qui souligna l'originalité des dessins bien qu'il ne lui ait pas attribué d'accessit. Sur la page précédente, une ébauche pour le même projet à côté d'un dessin préparatoire pour la tombe de Gerardo Caprotti (1914), pour le même cimetière.

Il progetto per il cimitero di Monza sorprese la giuria grazie alla originalità dei suoi disegni anche se non gli diedero nessun tipo di ricompensa. Nella pagina anteriore, uno schizzo del medesimo progetto insieme al disegno di preparazione per la tomba di Gerardo Caprotti (1914), nello stesso cimitero.

Cassa di Risparmio

Once he'd taken his diploma to work as an architect, in 1907, and moved to Milan, Sant'Elia began to collaborate with different architects, not only to earn his living but also to continue learning about his profession. The Canoti studio contracted him in mid-1913, along with the painter Leonardo Dureville, to design the new headquarters of the Verona savings bank, a building which was to be located on the Piazza delle Erbe, one of the most important in the city center. The end product of this project was an eclectic work that blended neo-Gothic components from the repertory of the north of Italy—e.g. the alternation of light-colored stones and dark-colored ones in the arches—with the preference of the Viennese Secession, such as the windows or the gilt facings. Sant'Elia will foresee here an exterior vision that realizes the most important features through a variety of solutions: one of the corners will be comprised of two perpendicular arches that form a portico, or a different roof to the zone making up the main entrance.

Nachdem er 1907 die Lizenz zur Berufsausübung erlangt hatte und nach Mailand gegangen war, arbeitete Sant'Elia mit verschiedenen Architekten zusammen, einerseits um seinen Lebensunterhalt zu bestreiten, andererseits, um den Berufsalltag kennenzulernen. Das Studio Canoti gab ihm Mitte 1913 den Auftrag, zusammen mit dem Maler Leonardo Dureville den neuen Sitz der Sparkasse in Verona zu entwerfen, welche auf der Piazza delle Erbe, einem der größten Plätze des Stadtzentrums liegen sollte. Der entstandene Entwurf war ein eklektisches Werk, das neugotische Elemente aus der mittelalterlichen Architektur Norditaliens, wie das Abwechseln heller und dunkler Steine bei den Bögen, mit Stilelementen der Wiener Secession mischte, wie z.B. Glasfenster oder goldene Verzierungen. Sant'Elia plante eine Außenansicht, die die wichtigsten Elemente durch verschiedene Lösungen hervorhebt: Eine der Ecken wurde durch zwei perpendikulare Bögen gebildet und gestaltete die Veranda, ein besonderes Dach findet sich im Bereich des Haupteingangs.

Après avoir obtenu son diplôme d'architecte, en 1907, et faisant suite à son déménagement pour Milan, Sant'Elia initia sa collaboration avec divers architectes, afin de subvenir à ses besoins mais aussi pour dans un souci d'apprentissage des réalités de sa profession. Le cabinet Canoti l'engagea au cours de l'année 1913 avec le peintre Leonardo Dureville, afin qu'il conçût le nouveau siège social de la caisse d'épargne de Vérone, qui devait occuper la Piazza delle Erbe, l'une des places les plus importantes du centre ville. Le projet eut pour résultante une œuvre éclectique mêlant les composants néo-gothiques du répertoire médiéval rencontrés dans le Nord de l'Italie, ainsi l'alternance de pierres claires et obscures pour les arches, avec la touche de la Secession viennoise pour les verrières ou les finitions dorées. Sant'Elia sut prévoir une vision extérieure rehaussant les éléments les plus importants au moyen de diverses solutions : un des angles composé de deux arches perpendiculaires donnant forme à un porche, ou une charpente distincte située dans la zone correspondant à l'entrée principale.

Da quando ottenne il titolo per lavorare come architetto nel 1907 e da quando si trasferì a Milano, Sant'Elia collaborò con diversi architetti, sia per mantersi sia per conoscere la realtà della professione. Lo studio Canoti lo contrattò nella metà del 1913 insieme al pittore Leonardo Dureville per disegnare la nuova sede della cassa di risparmio di Verona, che si sarebbe dovuta ubicare in Piazza delle Erbe, una delle più importanti del centro della città. Il progetto finale fu un'opera eclettica che mischiava componenti neogotiche del repertorio medioevale del nord Italia, come l'alternanza di pietra chiara e scura negli archi, con il gusto Secessionista Viennese, come le vetrate o i dettagli dorati. Sant'Elia seppe prevedere una visione esteriore di ciò che stava realizzando attraverso diverse soluzioni: uno degli angoli era caratterizzato mediante due archi prependicolari che davano forma a un patio, o una copertura che distingueva la zona corrispondente dall'entrata principale.

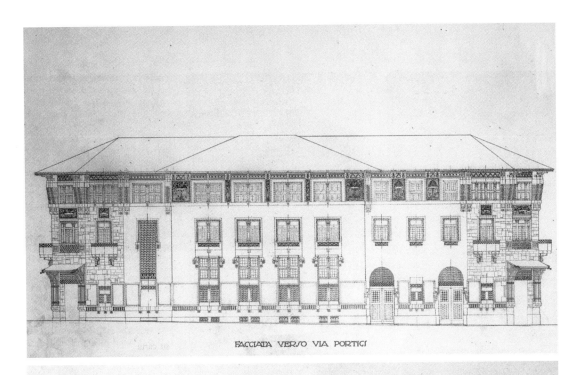

FACCIATA VERSO VIA PORTICI

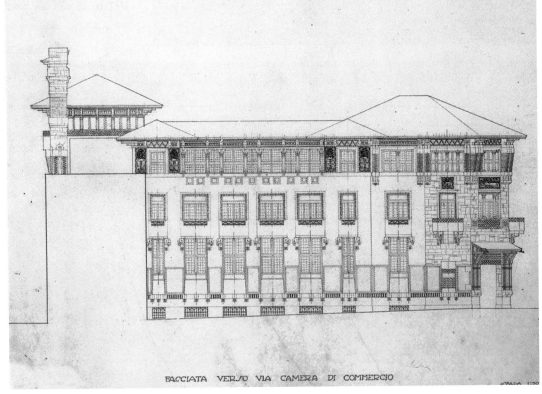

FACCIATA VERSO VIA CAMERA DI COMMERCIO

CONCORSO PER LA CASSA DI RISPARMIO DI VERONA

The blend of styles recalls both the building tradition of the north of Italy and the school of Otto Wagner.

Die Vermischung der Stile erinnert sowohl an die Bautradition Norditaliens als auch an die Schule Otto Wagners.

Le mariage des styles rappelle parfois la tradition architectonique du Nord de l'Italie mais aussi l'école d'Otto Wagner.

L'incrocio degli stili ricorda molto sia la tradizione costruttiva del nord Italia come la scuola di Otto Wagner.

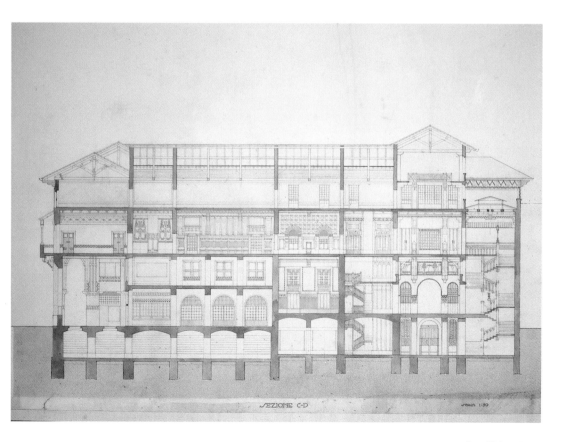

SEZIONE C-D   SCALA 1:50

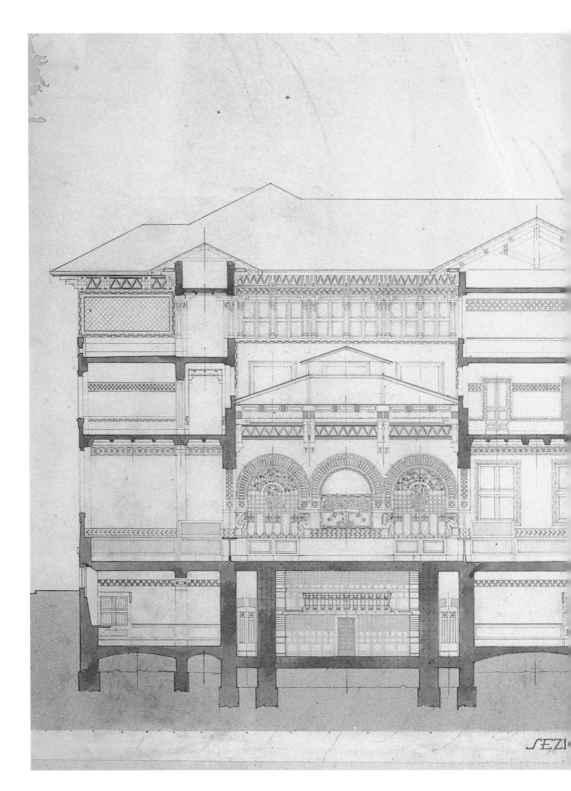

SEZI•

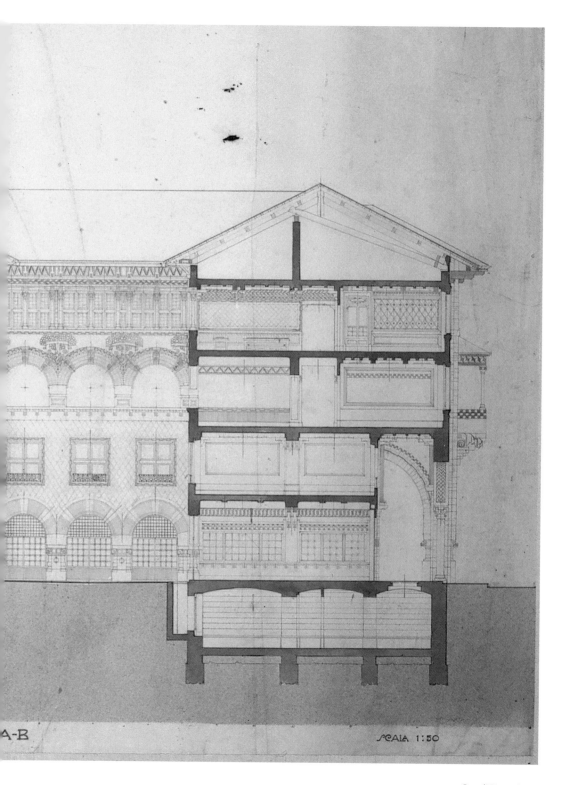

A-B

SCALA 1:50

Monumental Buildings

There is an extant series of drawings on which Sant'Elia began to work from 1909 onward and which the critics have classed together under the denomination of "monumental buildings". While it is difficult to establish their exact use, all of these works exhibit similar characteristics that allow them to be defined as exercises in composition. One of the interests they demonstrate is the control of a building's exterior hierarchy: large domes appear that jut out from the rest of the piece; staircases of a considerable degree of slope—and without a human scale—that establish perpendicular axes into powerful accessways; vast buttresses that transform the building into a tectonic mass that more closely resembles a lone pyramid than a structure destined to any urban use. In these sketches, you see the overlaps with the work of Wagner, whose most immediate reference point for domes, entrances with colossal staircases, or exorbitant perspectives is the Steinhof church. Wagner encouraged his students to work on fantasy projects to get them to give their imagination a workout. It is owing to the library of the Brera academy that the Como architect had access to the work of the students of Wagner, both to the pieces that were in fact realized and to the ones that remain architectural fantasies.

Es gibt eine Reihe von Zeichnungen, die Sant'Elia ab 1909 anfertigte und welche die Kritiker unter der Bezeichnung „monumentale Bauten" gruppiert haben. Obwohl es schwer fällt, deren Anwendung festzulegen, weisen doch alle ähnliche Merkmale auf und können damit als Stilübungen bezeichnet werden. Hier ist das Interesse zu sehen, die Hierarchie des Äußeren eines Volumens zu betonen: große Kuppeln, die sich vom Rest des Gebäudes abheben, Treppengänge mit markantem Schrägewinkel ohne menschlichen Maßstab, die aufsteigende Achsen zu großen Eingängen formen; grobe Strebepfeiler, die das Gebäude in eine tektonische Masse umformen, die eher einer Pyramide gleicht als einem Gebäude der Stadt. Bei diesen Skizzen ist der Einfluss der Werke Wagners zu erkennen. Dessen Kirche am Steinhof stellt, was Kuppeln, Aufgänge mit kolossalen Treppengängen oder übermäßige Perspektiven angeht, ein Musterbeispiel dar. Wagner ermunterte seine Schüler, an fantastischen Entwürfen zu arbeiten, um somit gezwungenermaßen ihre Vorstellungskraft zu fördern. Dank der Bibliothek der Akademie in Brera war der Architekt aus Como mit den Werken der Schüler Wagners vertraut, sowohl mit den tatsächlich verwirklichten Projekten als auch mit den architektonischen Fantasien.

Les critiques ont groupé sous la dénomination « d'édifices monumentaux » une série de croquis, initiée par Sant'Elia à partir de 1909. Bien que leur objet soit difficile à établir, tous présentent des caractéristiques similaires permettant de les définir comme des exercices de composition. La recherche de la maîtrise des hiérarchies extérieures d'un volume sont l'un des intérêts qu'ils présentent : grandes coupoles saillant du reste de la construction, des escaliers à l'inclinaison prononcée – dépourvus d'échelle humaine – établissant des axes ascendant vers des entrées magistrales, des arcs-boutants grossiers transforment le bâtiment en une masse tectonique, tenant plus d'une pyramide isolée que d'une construction urbaine. Ces ébauches laissent observer l'imbrication de l'œuvre de Wagner, dont le référent quant aux coupoles, aux accès offrant des escaliers colossaux ou des perspectives exorbitantes, est l'église du Steinhof. Wagner incitait ses élèves à travailler sur des projets, afin de les obliger à exercer leur imagination. Grâce à la bibliothèque de l'académie de Brera, l'architecte de Côme put accéder aux travaux des disciples de Wagner, tant aux projets concrétisés comme aux fantaisies architecturales.

Esistono una serie di disegni sui quali Sant'Elia iniziò a lavorare dal 1909 che vengono catalogati dai critici come "edifici monumentali". Anche se risulta difficile definirne lo scopo, tutti questi presentano delle caratteristiche simili che permettono di ricondurli a degli esercizi di composizione. Una delle motivazioni per l'interesse che suscitano si ritrova nella ricerca del predominio delle gerarchie esteriori di un volume: appaiono grandi cupole che fuoriescono dall'edificio, scalinate con una pendenza estremamente accentuata e senza scala umana, rozzi contrafforti che trasformano l'edificio in una massa tettonica, molto più simile ad una piramide isolata piuttosto che a una costruzione urbana. In questi schizzi si può notare una certa influenza dell'opera di Wagner, il punto di riferimento riguardo cupole, ingressi con maestose scalinate o prospettive esorbitanti come la chiesa di Steinhof. Wagner incoraggiava i suoi alunni nel lavorare in progetti fantastici per obbligarli nell'utilizzare l'immaginazione. Grazie alla biblioteca dell'accademia di Brera, l'architetto di Como seppe riconoscersi tra gli alunni di Wagner per la sua bravura sia nei progetti realizzati sia nei fantasie architettoniche.

The notable differences in grade and the domed towers clearly
refer to the work of the disciples of Otto Wagner, above all, the
architect Emil Hoppe

Die große Neigung und die Türme mit den Kuppeln sind
ganz deutlich an die Arbeiten der Schüler Otto Wagners
angelehnt, vor allem an die des Architekten Emil Hoppe

Les inclinaisons prononcées et les tours à coupole font
clairement référence aux œuvres des disciples d'Otto
Wagner, surtout celles de l'architecte Emil Hoppe

I forti pendi e le torri con cupole hanno un forte
riferimento alle opere dei seguaci di Otto Wagner
sopratutto dell'architetto Emil Hoppe

112

This drawing could be intended to represent a public building that gives onto a plaza. The sketch of a person walking, a very simple piece, contrasts with the drawing of people done some years earlier, which were much more elaborate.

Diese Zeichnung könnte ein öffentliches Gebäude darstellen, das auf einen Platz hinausgeht. Die sehr einfache Skizze einer laufenden Person kontrastiert mit Zeichnungen von Personen, die er einige Jahre zuvor angefertigt hatte und die erheblich mehr ausgearbeitet sind.

Ce dessin pourrait être destiné à un édifice public, car s'ouvrant sur une place. L'esquisse d'un badaud, très simplifiée, contraste avec les dessins des personnes quelques années plus tôt, bien plus fouillés.

Questo disegno potrebbe essere stato pensato per un edificio pubblico considerato che si apre una piazza difronte. Lo schizzo di una persona che cammina, molto semplice, contrasta con i disegni delle persone degli anni anteriori, molto più rielaborati.

For the drawings of monumental constructions the artist had recourse to already extant buildings such as this tower, which is not unreminiscent of the drawings of light beacons by Sant'Elia.

Für die Zeichnungen von monumentalen Gebäuden griff der Künstler auf bereits bestehende Gebäude zurück, wie z.B. bei diesem Turm, der an die Leuchtturmzeichnungen Sant'Elias erinnert.

Pour les dessins d'édifices monumentaux, l'auteur a recours aux constructions existants, comme cette tour, qui rappelle les esquisses de phares de Sant'Elia.

Per i disegni degli edifici monumentali l'autore ricorre agli esenti edifici, come questa torre che ricorda i disegni dei fari che ha Sant'Elia.

Electric Power Plants

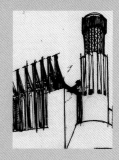

From the opening of the twentieth century, and from the beginning of the Industrial Age, the driving energies par excellence have been coal and gas. In the first decade of that century, electric energy rose up to become the symbol of modernization. The new city proposed by Sant'Elia instituted electricity as the driving force: from heavy equipment like that used in rail power to the utensils used in homes. It is not strange, then, that one of Sant'Elia's most often repeated designs was one for power stations. In spite of the somewhat diffuse definition in regard to technical characteristics, these drawings show some delimiting elements as to function, such as turbines, dams, and changes in grade as well as tension line installations beyond the building itself. The intent, then, is to establish a zero point for the electrical network linking city and energy source. The plans of Sant'Elia set out certain structures that are absolutely vast in their dimensions. Simple comparison with the station that supplied half of Milan at that time (the basis of the drawings' inspiration), allows us to see the architect's desire to design a much larger complex that could supply the needs of the modern city.

Seit Anfang des 20. Jahrhunderts und seit Anfang des Industriezeitalters waren Kohle und Gas die Bewegungsenergien schlechthin. Im ersten Jahrzehnt des vorigen Jahrhunderts wurde die elektrische Energie zum Symbol der Modernisierung erklärt. Die neue Weltstadt, die Sant'Elia propagierte, ernannte die Elektrizität zur treibenden Kraft, von den großen Anlagen für die Eisenbahn bis hin zu den Wohnbauten. Deshalb ist es nicht verwunderlich, dass die Elektrizitätswerke zu seinen meist wiederholten Entwürfen zählten. Auch wenn die technischen Merkmale nicht genauer definiert werden, sind in seinen Zeichnungen doch einige entscheidende funktionelle Elemente wie Turbinen, Staumauern und Gefälle zu sehen. Außerdem zeichnete er ein, wie Kabel verlegt sind, die über das Gebäude hinausgehen und somit eine Verbindung zwischen dem Elektrizitätsnetz und der Stadt herstellen. Die Pläne Sant'Elias zeigen absolut überdimensionierte Strukturen. Wenn wir sie mit dem Elektrizitätswerk vergleichen, das zu dieser Zeit halb Mailand versorgte und das der Ausgangspunkt für sein Projekt war, sehen wir die Absicht des Architekten, eine weit größere Anlage zu entwerfen, die es ermöglicht, den Bedarf der modernen Stadt zu decken.

Jusqu'à l'orée du XXème siècle, et dès les débuts de l'ère industrielle, le charbon et le gaz constituaient les énergies motrices par excellence. La première décennie du siècle voyait l'électricité s'ériger en symbole de la modernisation. La métropole nouvelle, dont Sant'Elia se faisait l'avocat, instituait l'électricité comme sa force motrice : des grands équipements, ainsi du chemin de fer, jusqu'aux logements mêmes. Il est donc peu surprenant que l'un des concepts les plus répétés fut celui des centrales électriques. En dépit de son manque de définition quant aux caractéristiques techniques, ses dessins permettent d'apprécier quelques éléments d'exposition de leur usage, comme des turbines, barrages et dénivellations, mais aussi de vastes réseaux de câbles se prolongeant bien au-delà d'un édifice, en une tentative d'établir le point de départ du réseau électrique faisant communiquer la centrale et la ville. Les schémas de Sant'Elia présentent des structures surdimensionnées : par comparaison avec la centrale approvisionnant alors la moitié de Milan, et qui constituait s'inspiration, l'on peut observer l'intention de concevoir un complexe conséquent, à même de répondre aux impératifs d'une ville moderne.

Sin dagli inizi del XX° secolo e al principio dell'era industriale, le energie motori che sono state per eccellenza quelle più importanti sono state quelle a carbone e a gas. Nel primo decennio l'energia elettrica incarna il simbolo della modernizzazione. La nuova urbe che promulgava Sant'Elia vedeva nell'elettricità la sua forza motrice: dalle infrastrutture come la ferrovia fino alle residenze. Non c'è da stupirsi quindi che uno dei disegni che ha ripetuto più volte fu quello delle centrali elettriche. A parte il significato di queste rispetto alle caratteristiche tecniche, nei suoi disegni si apprezzano alcuni elementi che definiscono un uso, come le turbine, le presse ed i livellatori, così come i grandi cavi di alta tensione che si prolungano oltre l'edificio, con l'intento di stabilire il punto iniziale della rete di elettricità che comunica la centrale con la città. Gli schemi di Sant'Elia raffigurano delle strutture sovradimensionate: se li si comparano con la centrale reale che riforniva mezza Milano in quell'epoca, che costituiva la base da cui si ispirò, si poteva capire l'intenzione dell'architetto nel disegnare un complesso molto più grande e capace di provvedere alle necessità della città moderna.

The electrical cables often define the use of these buildings, since the formal
setting is often the same as in many other depictions.

Die elektrischen Leitungen definieren oft die Funktion dieser Gebäude, gera-
de weil das formale Repertoire das gleiche wie in vielen
anderen Zeichnungen ist.

Les réseaux de câbles définissent souvent l'usage des constructions, le
répertoire formel étant similaire à celui de nombre d'autres dessins.

I cavi elettrici definiscono spesso la funzione di questi edifici, considerato
che il repertorio formale è lo stesso che in molti altri disegni.

The importance Sant'Elia will give electricity as the driving force of the modern city prompts him to design a series of power stations. They are notably larger than are those of the beginning of the twentieth century.

Die Wichtigkeit, die Sant'Elia der Elektrizität als Motor der modernen Stadt beimaß, veranlasste ihn, verschiedene Elektrizitätswerke zu zeichnen. Sie fielen dabei viel größer aus als sie Anfang des zwanzigsten Jahrhunderts tatsächlich waren.

L'importance accordée par Sant'Elia à l'électricité comme moteur de la ville moderne l'amène à concevoir diverses centrales électriques, bien plus grandes que celles existant aux débuts du XXème siècle.

L'importanza che Sant'Elia confiere alla elettricità come il motore della città moderna, gli permette di disegnare diverse centrali elettriche, molto grandi rispetto a quelle del principio del XX° secolo.

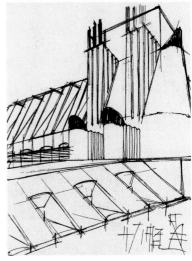

Architectural Elements

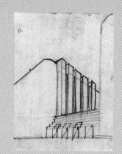

These drawings make up an interesting sample both of the way Sant'Elia worked and of one of his greatest aspirations (revealing an unadorned architectural compositional language where the forms were the building's sole protagonists). The greater part of the drawings are pencil sketches. They were only later redrawn in ink. No interest is visible in light or shade, which were included only in the color pieces, or in any of the buildings' potential apertures. Nor is there apparent the least inclination to define clearly a specific use. What we see instead are fragments, parts, volumes: the aim is to create a formal repertory that serves as basis for a language to build in concrete and steel. Conscious of the enormous possibilities still to be explored in these questions, Sant'Elia studies and imagines the forms that can be achieved with both these materials before considering the technical possibilities. This is the rational path chosen by the greater part of modern architects, people like Peter Behrens (1868–1940) who, in 1909, will design the turbine plant for AEG and, later, in 1911, the Frankfurter Gasgesellschaft factory. These will both comprise entities where the German architect develops his research in a way very close to that of the Italian.

Diese Zeichnungen bilden ein interessantes Beispiel sowohl der Arbeitsmethode Sant'Elias' als auch einer seiner größten Bestrebungen: eine kompositorische architektonische Formensprache ohne Dekoration zu finden, wobei die Formen die einzigen Protagonisten des Gebäudes sind. Größtenteils handelt es sich um Bleistiftskizzen, deren Umriss später mit Tinte nachgezeichnet wurde. Es ist keinerlei Interesse für Licht oder Schatten feststellbar (lediglich in den Farbzeichnungen sind Lichtverhältnisse eingezeichnet), noch für mögliche Öffnungen des Gebäudes. Ebenso ist keine Absicht zu erkennen, eine spezifische Funktion zu bestimmen. Es handelt sich um Fragmente, Teile, Volumen, deren Ziel die Ausarbeitung eines Formenrepertoires war, das als Basis für eine Formensprache zur Konstruktion mit Beton und Eisen dienen sollte. Sich der enormen, unerforschten Möglichkeiten dieser Materialien bewusst, begann Sant'Elia die Formen, die damit erzielt werden können, zu erforschen und zu planen, bevor er deren technische Möglichkeiten in Erwägung zog. Dies war der vernünftigste Weg, den die Mehrheit der modernen Architekten wählte, wie Peter Behrens (1868–1940), der 1909 das Turbinenwerk von AEG und 1911 das Gebäude der Frankfurter Gasgesellschaft entwarf, Bauten, bei denen der Deutsche eine dem Italiener ähnliche Studie vornahm.

Ces dessins composent un exemple de la méthode de Sant'Elia et l'un des ses principaux attraits : découvrir un langage architectural dépouillé où les formes sont l'unique acteur de l'édifice. La plupart des esquisses sont réalisée au crayon, ensuite redessinées à l'encre ; aucun intérêt pour la lumière ou l'ombre n'est patent – seulement en filigrane pour les dessins de couleur – ni pour les ouvertures des constructions. De même, aucune inclination envers la définition claire d'un usage spécifique n'est notable : ce sont des fragments, parties et volumes ; l'objectif est l'élaboration d'un répertoire formel offrant une base de langage pour les constructions en béton et en métal. Conscient des vastes possibilités encore inexplorées de ces matériaux, Sant'Elia étudie et imagine les formes susceptibles d'être obtenues avec ces composants, avant d'en considérer les possibilités techniques. Il s'agit pourtant du cheminement rationnel de la majorité des architectes modernes comme Peter Behrens (1868–1940), concevant en 1909 l'usine de turbines d'AEG et, en 1911, celle de la Frankfurter Gasgesellschaft, pour lesquelles l'Allemand développa une recherche très similaire à celle de l'Italien.

Questi disegni rappresentano un'interessante rassegna del modo di lavorare di Sant'Elia: trovare un linguaggio compositivo architettonico dove le forme costituivano l'unico protagonista dell'edificio. La maggior parte sono schizzi a matita il cui contorno venne ripassato con china; non si avverte nessun interesse per la luce o l'ombra – solo accennata nei disegni a colore – neppure per le aperture dell'edificio. Così come non si osserva neppure nessuna inclinazione per definire la funzione dell'edificio: sono frammenti, parti, volumi; l'obiettivo è elaborare un repertorio formale che possa servire come base di un linguaggio per la costruzione in cemento e in ferro. Cosciente delle possibilità dei materiali non ancora esplorate, Sant'Elia studia e immagina le forme che si possono ricavare con i componenti prima ancora di considerare le loro potenzialità tecniche, caratteristica del cammino razionale che intrapresero la maggior parte degli architetti moderni, come Peter Behrens (1868–1940), che disegnò nel 1909 la fabbrica delle turbine dell'AEG, nel 1911 la fabbrica della Frankfurter Gasgesellschaft, costruzioni dove l'architetto tedesco sviluppò una ricerca molto simile a quella dell'italiano.

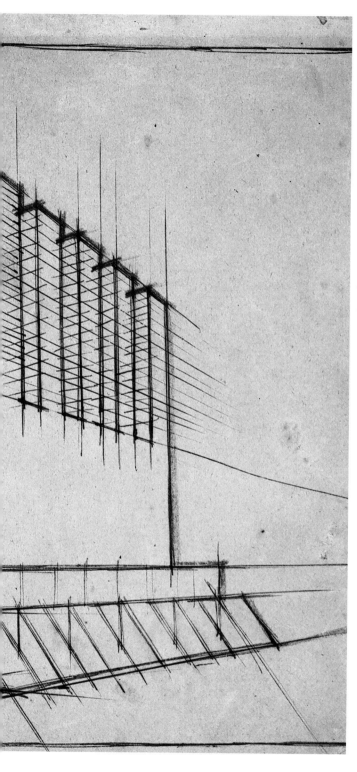

In no small number of these pictures, the interest resides in the forms that stress the architectural monumentality, which evokes factories. Here, a large staircase forms the accessway, while the buttressing pieces establish a striking fundamental rhythm in both walls.

Das Interesse vieler dieser Zeichnungen liegt bei den Formen, die das Monumentale in der Architektur unterstreichen und die an Fabriken erinnern. In dieser Skizze bildet eine Freitreppe den Aufgang, während die Strebepfeiler einen kräftigen und grundlegenden Rhythmus in den beiden Mauern aufbauen.

L'intérêt de nombre de ces dessins réside dans quelques formes rehaussant la monumentalité architectonique, rappelant notamment les usines. Dans ce dessin, un grand escalier marque un accès, alors que les arcs-boutants établissent un rythme basique et définitif pour les deux parois.

L'interesse di molti di questi disegni risiede nelle forme che risaltano la monumentalità architettonica, forme che ricordano quelle delle fabbriche. In questo disegno una grande scalinata definisce l'ingresso, mentre i contrafforti stabiliscono un ritmo base e ben marcato in ambi i muri.

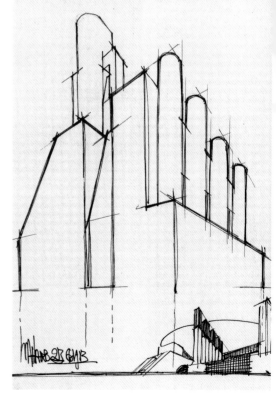

Industrial Buildings

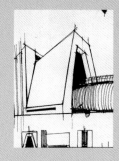

The construction of large manufactory structures had begun some years earlier in Germany, France, and England, and it was starting to extend to Italy, precisely, by way of Milan. In the context of the time, these large complexes are identifiable with heavy industry, which needed many adjacent infrastructures. As in his power plant designs, Sant'Elia here also shows an intention to monumentalize the machine and its industry: the drawings are in no way ambiguous in regard to the wish to create a generic type of factory under the obvious influence of Tony Garnier. Sant'Elia will take advantage of elements like the large deposits or the powerful buttresses of these complexes to create his expressive solutions. But many of these sketches lack the human scale, the resource inherited from the tradition of architecture designed without the intention of building, that represented by Piranesi, Boulée, and Ledoux. These plans respond to the will of the architect to do the modern city project. But in spite of Sant'Elia's not developing a theory of urbanism, he still worked with the desire to create the spaces of this new metropolis, electric, monumental, well served by transportation systems.

Der Bau großer Fabrikgebäude hatte einige Jahre zuvor in Deutschland, Frankreich und England begonnen und breitete sich über Mailand in Italien aus. Innerhalb dieses Zeitalters waren diese großen Komplexe mit der Schwerindustrie gleichzusetzen, für die zahlreiche anliegende Infrastrukturen benötigt wurden. Ebenso wie bei den Entwürfen der Elektrizitätswerke beabsichtigte Sant'Elia Maschine und Industrie zu monumentalisieren. In seinen Zeichnungen ist deutlich das Interesse zu erkennen, unter dem Einfluss von Tony Garnier eine einheitliche Fabrikarchitektur zu schaffen. Sant'Elia nutzte Elemente wie große Lagerhallen oder gewaltige Strebepfeiler dieser Komplexe um seine Ausdrucksformen zu erlangen. Jedoch fehlt bei vielen seiner Skizzen der menschliche Maßstab, ein Mittel, das er von einer Architekturströmung übernahm, die ohne konstruktive Absicht plante und die durch Piranesi, Boulée und Ledoux vertreten wurde. Diese Abrisse entsprechen der Absicht des Architekten, die moderne Stadt zu projektieren; obwohl Sant'Elia es nicht so weit brachte, eine urbanistische Theorie zu entwickeln, so versuchte er doch, die Flächen dieser neuen elektrischen, monumentalen und mit gutem Verkehrsnetz versehenen Weltstadt zu gestalten.

La construction de grandes structures de production avait déjà quelques années d'existence en Allemagne, en France et en Angleterre et s'étendait à l'Italie, précisément via Milan. Dans le contexte d'alors, ces vastes complexes s'identifient à l'industrie lourde, requérant de multiples infrastructures adjacentes. À l'unisson de ses croquis de centrales électriques, Sant'Elia montre une intention de monumentaliser la machine et l'industrie : ses dessins permettent d'apprécier l'intérêt envers la création d'un type générique d'usine, sous l'influence de Tony Garnier. Sant'Elia met à profit les éléments comme les grands dépôts ou les puissantes travées de ces complexes pour créer ses solutions d'expression. Pour autant, nombre d'esquisses sont dépourvues d'échelle humaine, une pratique héritée de la tradition d'architecture conceptuelle sans intention constructive, représentée par Piranesi, Boulée et Ledoux. Ces schémas répondent à la volonté de l'architecte de projeter la ville moderne. Bien que Sant'Elia n'ait pas eu le temps de développer une théorie urbanistique, il put cependant prétendre à la création des espaces de cette nouvelle métropole électrique, monumentale et communiquant parfaitement.

La costruzione delle fabbriche era iniziata alcuni anni prima in Germania, Francia e Inghilterra e incominciava ad espandersi in Italia precisamente a partire e grazie a Milano. Nel contesto dell'epoca, questi grandi complessi si identificavano con l'industria che caratterizzava numerose infrastrutture adiacenti. Come nei disegni delle centrali elettriche, Sant'Elia dimostra l'intenzione di monumentalizzare la macchina e l'industria: nei suoi disegni si apprezza l'interesse nel creare un genere di fabbrica generico sotto la chiara influenza di Tony Garnier. Sant'Elia aprofitta gli elementi convertendoli in grandi depositi o in contrafforti di questi complessi per creare le sue soluzioni espressive. Tuttavia in molti dei suoi bozzetti manca la figura umana, escamotage ereditato dall'architettura senza fine costruttivo, rappresentato da Piranesi, Boulée e Ledoux. Questi schemi rispondono alla volontà dell'architetto di progettare la città moderna; anche se Sant'Elia non arrivò a sviluppare nessuna teoria urbanistica, pretese di creare gli spazi di questa nuova metropoli monumentale e ben connessa.

The bodies and the coordination among the parts are the main things that interest Sant'Elia when he does these sketches. And the use of perspective is never absent from the drawing.

Der Rauminhalt und die Koordinierung der Teile sind die Themen, die ihn beim Realisieren dieser Skizzen, welche immer in Perspektive gezeichnet sind, interessieren.

Les volumes et la coordination entre les parties sont les thèmes qui l'attirent lorsqu'il réalise ces ébauches, toujours dessinées en perspective.

I volumi e la coordinazione tra le parti sono i temi che gli interessano quando realizza questi schizzi, disegnando sempre in prospettiva.

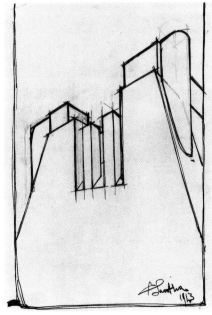

The manufactories needed large warehouses and hangars, also foreseen by Sant'Elia. The use of the Zeppelin was common in this period, and the large hangars of airports doubtless influenced the work of the Como architect.

Die Fabriken benötigten große Lager und Flugzeughallen, welche von Sant'Elia auch vorausgesehen wurden. Der Gebrauch des Zeppelins war in dieser Epoche üblich und die großen Flugzeughallen der Flughäfen beeinflussten sicherlich das Werk des Architekten aus Como.

Les usines nécessitent également de grands entrepôts et hangars, eux aussi prévus par Sant'Elia. L'utilisation du dirigeable était répandue à l'époque et les vastes hangars des aéroports ont certainement influencé l'œuvre de l'architecte de Côme.

Le fabbriche necessitano anche di grandi magazzini e hangar, previsti anche da Sant'Elia. L'uso del Zeppelin aero comune in quest'epoca, ed i grandi hangar degli aeroporti influenzarono sicuramente il lavoro dell'architetto di Como.

Large factory constructions for heavy industry were altering the landscape of a good number of European cities. These buildings greatly interested Sant'Elia because of the modernity they represented and their use of concrete and steel.

Die großen Bauwerke der Schwerindustrie veränderten die bauliche Landschaft vieler europäischer Städte. Sant'Elia war sehr an ihnen interessiert, weil sie Modernität ausstrahlten und Eisen und Beton beim Bau verwendet wurden.

Les grandes constructions d'usines de l'industrie lourde commencent à modifier le paysage de beaucoup de cités européennes et ont notablement intéressé Sant'Elia, de par la modernité qu'elles représentent et en raison des matériaux employés, le béton et le fer.

Le grandi costruzioni delle fabbriche di industria pesante stavano trasformando il paesaggio di molte città europee, e interessarono molto Sant'Elia, per la modernità che rappresentavano e per essere costruite con cemento e ferro.

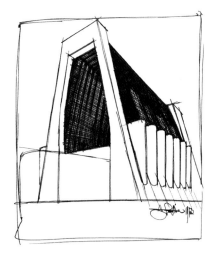

Theaters

Sant'Elia studied the typology of theater in different drawings. Along with the movie theaters he did, the live stage of the beginning of the last century already constituted one of city society's entertainment centers. Simple though the sketches may appear, they show a growing interest to establish a relationship between inside/outside. The orchestra seats, which inside appear empty, will translate outside into a metallic cladding with clerestories that work like large lanterns, while the untextured exterior walls will translate inside into the accessway to the theater itself. This power play establishes itself on the basis of a perspectival elevation with a simple twin counterpart that consists of an associated ground plan. The Como architect's pictures make it possible for viewers to discern a relationship between use and form. They constitute an application of the architectural forms established per se on a blueprint of a concrete case. Much less monumental than in other projects and thus all the more surprising is the solution given to the apertures.

Sant'Elia fertigte in verschiedenen Zeichnungen Studien zur Typologie des Theaters an, da dieses sich neben den Kinosälen schon Anfang des vorigen Jahrhunderts als eine der Unterhaltungsstätten der urbanen Gesellschaft abzeichnete. Trotz der Schlichtheit dieser Zeichnungen ist auf diesen Skizzen ein wachsendes Interesse zu sehen, ein Verhältnis zwischen Innen- und Außenraum herzustellen. Das Parkett, dessen Inneres nichtssagend ist, verwandelt sich außen in eine Metallstruktur mit Glaselementen, die als große Oberlichter fungieren, gleichzeitig verwandelt sich der glatte Außenteil im Inneren zum Saaleingang. Dieses Verhältnis konnte durch einen Aufriss der Perspektive erreicht werden, der einen sehr einfach strukturierten Grundriss hervorbringt. Diese Skizzen sind die einzigen des Architekten aus Como, die einen Zusammenhang zwischen Zweckmäßigkeit und Form erkennen lassen und bilden die Anwendung architektonischer Formen auf ein konkretes Gebäude. Überraschend ist die Lösung für die Zugänge, die hier weitaus weniger monumental sind als bei anderen Projekten.

Sant'Elia a étudié la typologie du théâtre dans plusieurs dessins. En effet, et à l'instar des salles de cinéma, celui-ci apparaissait dès le début du XXième siècle comme l'un des centres de loisirs de la société urbaine. En dépit de leur simplicité, les esquisses laissent observer un intérêt croissant envers l'établissement d'une relation entre les espaces intérieur et extérieur. L'orchestre, qui peut sembler vide puis l'intérieur, se traduit à l'extérieur en une structure métallique dont les fenêtres fonctionnent comme de grandes claires-voies, de la même manière que la partie extérieure lisse se traduit, à l'intérieur, en un accès à la salle. Cette relation a pu être établie sur le fondement d'une élévation en perspective allant de paire avec un niveau, bien que simplifié. Ces ébauches sont les seules de l'architecte de Côme permettant de discerner une relation entre l'usage et la forme. Ainsi, elles constituent une application des formes architecturales, dessinées per se, à un cas concret. La solution offerte aux accès surprend de par une monumentalité moins importante que pour d'autres projets.

Sant'Elia studiò la tipologia del teatro in diversi disegni, considerato che, insieme alle sale cinematografiche, si profilava all'inizio del secolo XX come uno dei centri di intrattenimento della società urbana. Non ostante la semplicità dei suoi disegni, si osserva negli schizzi un crescente interesse nello stabilire una relazione tra spazio interno ed esterno. La platea, che all'interno appare vuota, si traduce verso l'esterno come una struttura metallica con vetri che hanno la funzione di grandi lucernai, e allo stesso tempo la parte esteriore liscia si traduce all'interno nell'accesso alla sala. Questa relazione ha potuto permettersi partendo da una facciata in prospettiva che si fa riferimento, anche se in modo molto semplificato, a una pianta. Questi schizzi sono gli unici dell'architetto di Como che permettono di discernere una relazione tra funzione e forma, e costituiscono un'applicazione delle forme architettoniche disegnate per se in un caso concreto. Sorprende la soluzione delle entrate, molto meno monumentali che in altri progetti.

The line in this drawing is much more fully defined than in others. The architect's language, now more assured, serves here to delineate the basic features of a theater in a more finished way than in many of his other pictures.

Die Grundlinien dieser Zeichnung sind bestimmter ausgeführt als in den anderen. Die Sprache des Architekten betont hier die grundlegenden Merkmale eines Theaters deutlicher als dies in anderen Skizzen und Zeichnungen der Fall ist.

Le profil de ce dessin est bien plus défini que pour d'autres. Le langage de l'architecte, affirmé, sert ici à définir les caractéristiques de base d'un théâtre, bien plus précis que nombre de ses ébauches et dessins.

Il profilo di questo disegno è molto più definito degli altri. Il linguaggio dell'architetto, maturo, serve qui per definire le caratteristiche basiche di un teatro, maggiormente definito che molti altri suoi schizzi o disegni.

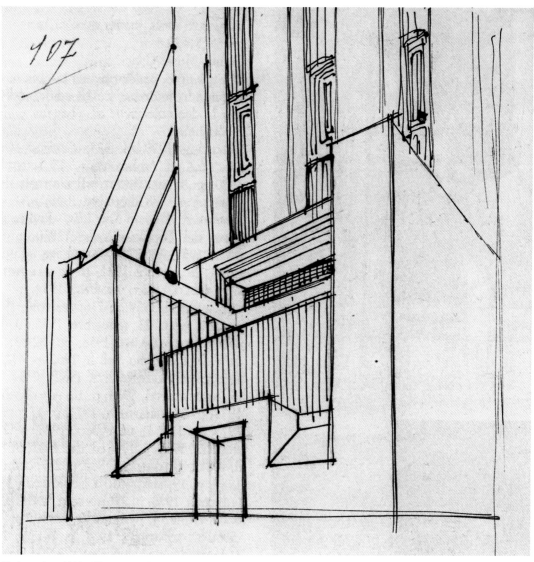

The interest in establishing different models of theaters seems clear.
The drawings are highly perfected, as witness the one on the right,
where different elevations define the project in a more finished way.

Das Interesse, verschiedene Theatermodelle darzustellen, erscheint klar. Die
Zeichnungen wie beispielsweise jene auf der rechten Seite sind sehr detail-
liert ausgeführt, wobei verschiedene Aufrisse das Projekt noch exakter
beschreiben.

L'intérêt envers la création de divers modèles de théâtre semble évident,
avec des dessins relativement fouillés, comme celui de droite. Apparaissent
en effet diverses élévations définissant plus avant le projet.

**L'interesse nello stabilire differenti modelli di teatri sembra evidente,
mediante disegni abbastanza definiti, come a destra, dove appaiono
differenti prospetto che definiscono molto di più il progetto.**

La Città Nuova

The series of drawings for "La Città Nuova", a global project that was never published as such but that does appear in the 1914 Futurist manifesto, shows how, in spite of being isolated buildings, they stem from the same ideation of city. The communications and the power lines are the protagonists of the metropolis and at the same time cement and steel are the leading actors of the buildings themselves. Sant'Elia finds his place as a visionary when he creates a large communications center with an airport forty years before the commercial use of the airplane. Moreover, accompanying this work is the proposal of wireless telegraph lines as an element in the story, thus anticipating today's omnipresent telecommunications. But even more revolutionary is the block of flats with terrace, based on ideas of the French architect Henri Sauvage (1873–1932). Sant'Elia will foresee elevators traveling through the façade as a way of taking advantage of more inside surface. He will seek formulas to ventilate all of the apartments and provide them with a sunwashed terrace. Electricity runs not only the lifts but also the lighted sign on the roof, still another element that surprises us in its anticipation of the city panorama we are living in.

Die Serie von Zeichnungen über die „Città Nuova" (ein globales Projekt, das nie als solches veröffentlicht wurde, aber im futuristischen Manifest von 1914 enthalten ist) zeigt, dass die Gebäude, obwohl sie voneinander getrennt sind, ein und derselben Stadtvision angehören. Verkehrswege und Elektrizität sind die Hauptfiguren der großen Weltstadt, Zement und Eisen die ihrer Gebäude. Sant'Elia war seiner Zeit voraus, er plante ein riesiges Zentrum der Verkehrsverbindungen mit eigenem Flughafen, vierzig Jahre bevor Flugzeuge übliche Transportmittel wurden, und schlug als eines der unabdingbaren Elemente drahtlose Telegrafenmäste vor, wodurch er der aktuellen Allgegenwart der Fernmeldetechnik zuvorkam. Noch revolutionärer jedoch ist der Wohnblock mit Terrasse, der auf Ideen des französischen Architekten Henri Sauvage (1873–1932) basiert. Sant'Elia sah Aufzüge an der Fassade vor, damit die Innenräume besser genutzt werden, und versuchte, alle Wohnungen weiträumig und mit einer sonnigen Terrasse anzulegen. Sowohl die Aufzüge als auch das Leuchtschild auf dem Dach – erstaunlich diese Antizipation der heutigen Stadtlandschaft – werden mit Elektrizität gespeist.

La série de dessins appartenant à la « Città Nuova », un projet global qui ne fut jamais publié comme tel mais apparaît dans le manifeste futuriste de 1914, démontre que, bien qu'ils constituent des immeubles isolées, ils forment partie du même concept citadin. Les communications et l'électricité sont les protagonistes de la grande métropole, tout comme le ciment et le fer pour les constructions. Sant'Elia s'érige en visionnaire, projetant un grand centre de communications avec aéroport, quarante ans avant l'aventure commerciale de l'avion, mais aussi en proposant comme éléments indispensables les antennes de télégraphie sans fil, anticipant l'omniprésence contemporaine des télécommunications. Cependant, la révolution profonde naît des blocs d'appartements avec terrasse – inspirés par les idées de l'architecte français Henri Sauvage (1873–1932) – et prévoyant des ascenseurs en façade afin de profiter plus avant la surface intérieure tout en recherchant des formules afin que tous les logements soient correctement ventilés et disposent d'une terrasse ensoleillée. L'électricité alimente les ascenseurs mais aussi l'enseigne lumineuse du toit, un élément qui surprend par son anticipation du panorama urbain contemporain.

La serie dei disegni appartenenti alla "Città Nuova", progetto globale che venne mai pubblicato in originale ma appare nel manifesto futurista del 1914, dimostrano che, non ostante il fatto che sono edifici isolati, appartengono alla stessa idea di città. Le comunicazioni e l'elettricità sone le protagoniste della grande metropoli, considerato il fatto che il cemento ed il ferro lo sono dei suoi edifici. Sant'Elia si dichiara visionario nel progettare un grande centro di comunicazioni con aeroporto quarant'anni prima dell'uso commerciale dell'aereo, e anche nel proporre come elemento indispensabile le antenne del telegrafo senza fili, che anticipa la attuale onnipresenza delle telecomunicazioni. Tuttavia appare più rivoluzionario il blocco di appartamenti con terrazza – pensato sull'idea dell'architetto Henri Sauvage (1873–1932) – che anticipa gli ascensori sulle facciate al fine di approfittare il più possibile la superficie interna, trovando soluzioni affinché tutti gli appartamenti siano areati e abbiano una terrazzo soleggiata. La elettricità alimenta tanto i ascensori come il rotolo luminoso delle terrazze, elementi che sorprendono per il loro anticipo al panorama urbano attuale.

This drawing featured in the Futurist Architecture Manifesto is one
of Sant'Elia's most well-known sketches, which shows the elements
that best define his vision of the city.

Diese Zeichnung, welche in dem Manifest für futuristische Architektur
veröffentlicht wurde, ist eine der berühmtesten Sant'Elias, weil in ihr die
Elemente, welche seine Ideen von einer Stadt erklären,
erscheinen.

Ce dessin, publié dans le Manifeste de l'architecture futuriste, est l'un des
plus célèbre de Sant'Elia et l'on peut y noter les éléments qui définissent sa
conception de la cité.

**Questo disegno pubblicato nel Manifesto dell'Architettura Futurista è uno
dei più famosi di Sant'Elia, dove appaiono già gli elementi che definiscono
la sua idea di città.**

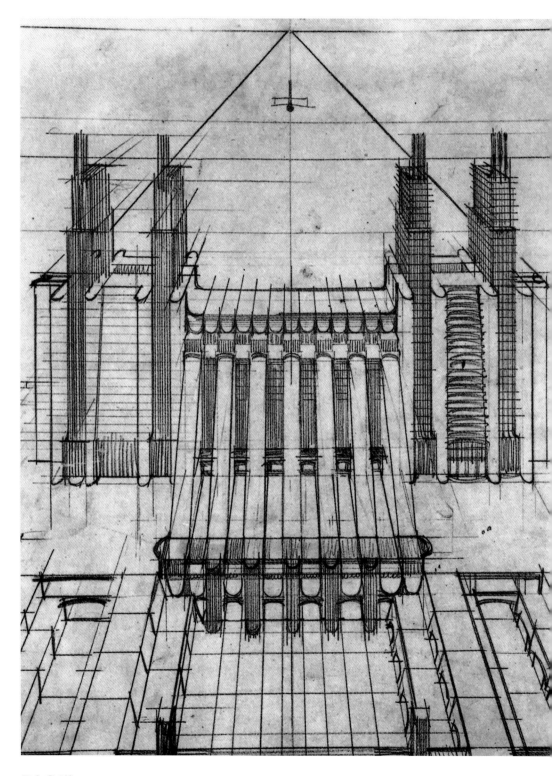

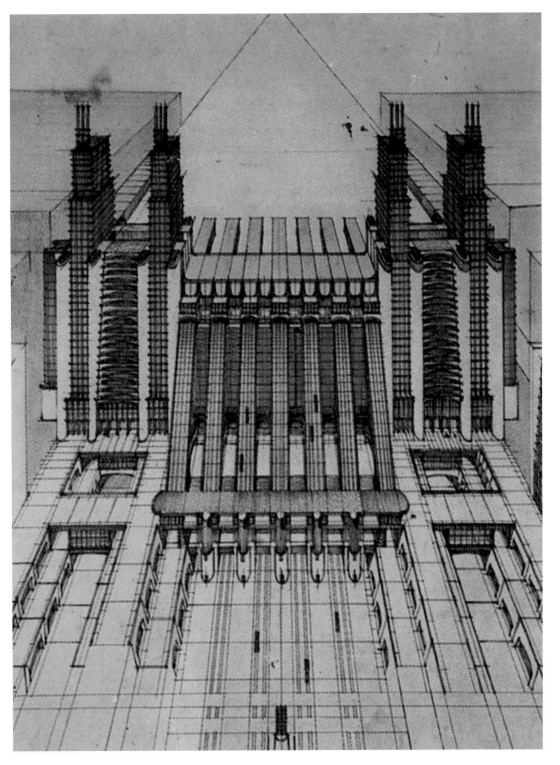

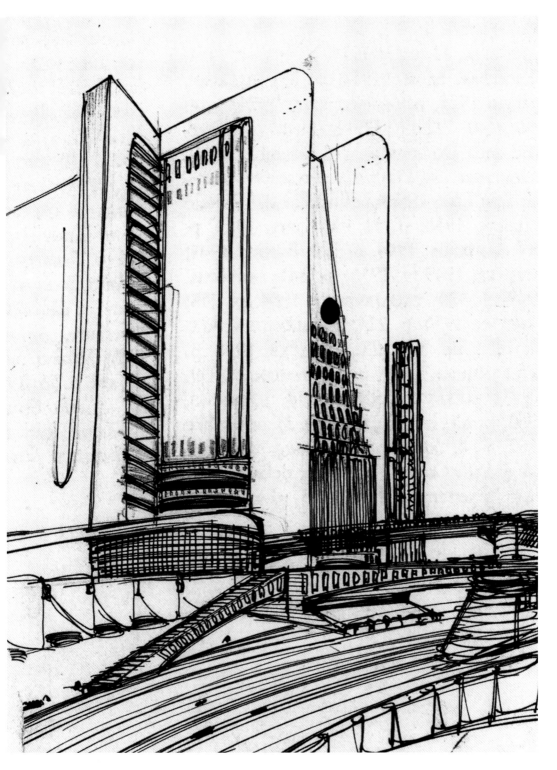

Metropolitan Churches

For Sant'Elia, churches were a very important part of the city. In almost every one of the architect's sketches, the accessways are monumental: a large staircase delineates an entry of very pronounced symbolic function. Flanking this, at times on the façade itself, cyclopean sculptures appear to magnify even further the Catholic tradition of using sculptures to ornament the outside of its temples. The nave inside becomes a space of powerful buttresses, in the form of arches or of triangular pieces, a move that confers different plastic solutions on a single function. The aim of these pictures is concentrated on the façades: in very few of them does the viewer find a desire to create a solution for the transept or for the main altar, and these are spaces that usually stand out. The ways Wagner and Hoppe have set out are visible in these plans. This is true above all in the manner in which the staircases rise up, and in the sculptural repertory—in spite of the fact that we do not find it in the dome—a solution much employed by the Viennese architects, and one which Sant'Elia himself uses in other pieces.

Für Sant'Elia waren Kirchen ein sehr wichtiger Bestandteil der Städte. Auf fast allen Skizzen des Architekten sind die Aufgänge monumental: ein großer Treppengang markiert eine betont aufsteigende Linie mit einer klaren symbolischen Funktion. Das Eingangstor flankierend, manchmal auch an der Fassade, erscheinen zyklopische Skulpturen, wodurch der katholischen Tradition, die Außenseite der Kirche mit Skulpturen zu schmücken, Rechnung getragen wird. Das Schiff geht außen in gewaltige Strebepfeiler in Form von Bögen oder Dreiecken über, was derselben Funktion verschiedene plastische Lösungen verleiht. Bei diesen Zeichnungen liegt der Schwerpunkt auf der Fassade und nur bei wenigen ist ein Interesse für das Querhaus oder den Hochaltar zu erkennen, die gewöhnlich hervorgehoben werden. Die Lehren Wagners und Hoppes sind in diesen Konzepten gegenwärtig, vor allem in der aufsteigenden Linie der Treppen und im plastischen Repertoire, obwohl auf Kuppeln verzichtet wird, eine von den Wiener Architekten häufig angewandte Lösung, auf die Sant'Elia selbst bei anderen Zeichnungen zurückgriff.

Pour Sant'Elia, les églises constituent l'un des éléments importants des cités. Dans la quasi totalité des esquisses, les accès en sont monumentaux : un grand escalier marque une ligne d'accès ascendante très prononcée, arborant une claire fonction symbolique. De part et d'autre de l'entrée, parfois en façade, apparaissent des sculptures cyclopéennes qui permettent de magnifier d'autant plus la tradition catholique d'ornementation avec des sculptures à l'extérieur des temples. La nef se traduit à l'extérieur par des arcs-boutants colossaux, en formes d'arcs ou de triangles, conférant diverses solutions plastiques à la même fonction. L'intérêt de ces dessins est essentiellement concentré dans les façades. Peu d'entre eux laissent apprécier un souci pour la création d'une réponse pour le transept ou l'autel principal, traditionnellement relevés. Les enseignements de Wagner et de Hoppe sont présents dans ces plans, surtout quant à l'ascension des escaliers et au répertoire sculptural et en dépit du fait qu'il n'ait pas recours à la coupole, une solution de prédilection pour les Viennois et que Sant'Elia lui même utilise dans d'autres croquis.

Per Sant'Elia le chiese erano considerate un elemento molto importante delle città. In quasi tutti gli schizzi le entrate sono monumentali: una grande scalinata definisce una linea molto pronunciata di accesso ascendente con una chiara funzione simbolica. Costeggiando l'entrata, nella facciata, in modo discontinuo appaiono sculture ciclopiche che enfatizzano ancor di più la tradizione cattolica nella decorazione con sculture le parti esteriori dei templi. La navata si traduce in esterno mediante poderosi contrafforti, con forme di archi o di triangoli, simboli che caratterizzano differenti soluzioni plastiche mantenendo la stessa funzione. L'interesse di questi disegni é concentrato nelle facciate, e si denota uno scarso interesse nella progettazione di nuove forme per il transetto o per l'altare maggiore, che era solito realizzarsi. Gli insegnamenti di Wagner e di Hoppe sono presenti in questi schemi, soprattutto nella ascensione delle scale e el repertorio scultoreo, anche se non si utilizza la cupola, una soluzione molto sfruttata dai viennesi e dallo stesso Sant'Elia in altri disegni.

Arch. ANTONIO SANT'ELIA

Chronology of Sant'Elia's works

1888	Birth, April 30, in Como, Italy.
1903	Diploma from the Cantù Technical School, Cantù, Italy; entry into Castellani Industrial Arts School, Como, Italy. He specialized in civil and hydraulic construction and other subjects.
1906	Completes his studies in Como, Italy.
1907	Moves to Milan, Italy, where he begins to work as an architectural draftsman in the technical office of the Milan Town Hall.
1909	Matriculates in the Academy of Brera, Italy.
1910	Project "Villino Moderno" presented to the Cooperativa Milanino competition (for the construction of a city garden). Published in "Il villino moderno. Racolta di proggeti per il concorso omonimo", 1911, Como, Italy.
1911	Participates with Italo Paternoster, a fellow student in Brera, in the international competition offered for the new cemetery for Monza, Italy.
1912	Builds the Villa Elisi, a small summer house in Le Colme, on the outskirts of Brunate, Italy. (Later renovated without much respect for the original project).
	Project for the central station, Milan, Italy.
1913	Project for the Cassa di Risparmio on the Piazza Delle Erbe, Verona, Italy.

1914	National competition for the new parish church of Salsomaggiore, Italy.
	Exhibition of his drawings of the Città Nuova in the Nuove Tendenze group, Milan, Italy.
	In July, the "Manifesto dell'architettura futurista" is published in pamphlet form and later included in the August number of the magazine "Lacerba".
	Stands in the municipal elections of Como for the socialists and is elected a member of the communal council.
	Funerary monument for the tomb of Signor Caprotti, in the cemetery of San Gregorio. Years later, this would be moved to the central cemetery of Monza, which occasioned some modifications.
1915	Enlists in the Lombard Volunteer Bicycle Battalion, where other members of the Futurist group such as Marinetti and Russolo had also enlisted.
1916	Draws the project for the war cemetery for the Arezzo Brigade, where he will be buried.
	Death at the front, 10 October, in Montfalcone, Italy.
1921	His body is moved to the main cemetery of Como, Italy.

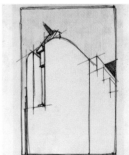